C000161011

PIE FORTUNE and the EVIL WIZARD

PIE
FORTUNE
and the
EVIL
WIZARD

Gareth P Jones

Dan Whisker

Collins

Contents

The Kingdom of Mirthia

The Great City – surrounded by *Lovely Woodland*

Big Pond Lake is to the west where the *Trout Tickling Tribes* live on a floating village.

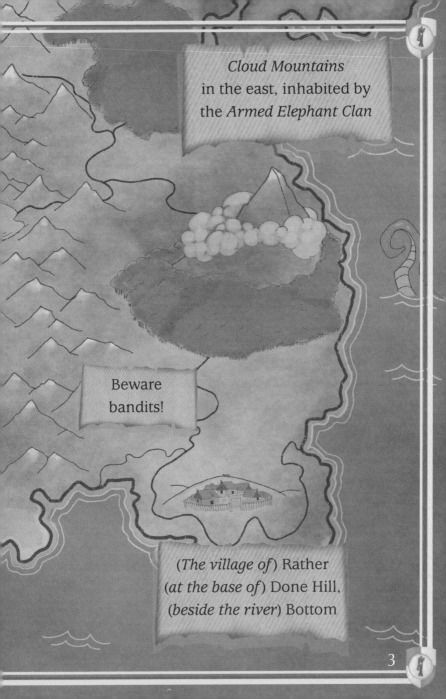

Cloud Mountains
in the east, inhabited by
the *Armed Elephant Clan*

Beware
bandits!

(*The village of*) Rather
(*at the base of*) Done Hill,
(*beside the river*) Bottom

Chapter 1

Lovely Woodland walks

"*Lovely Woodland* walks!"

The panicked cry came from the top
of the lookout tower in the east corner of
the Great City. Down below, the two city guards
looked at each other.

"I wonder what that means," said Pie.

"He's probably talking about the many walks that can be enjoyed in our surrounding forest," replied MacDuffy. "After all, it is called *Lovely Woodland* and it does have some charming walks. You do have to mind out for bandits, but the bluebells are stunning this time of year."

"I don't think he would have sounded quite so terrified if that's what he meant." Pie propped his spear against the city wall and looked up at the tower. The lookout was waving frantically and screaming the words "*Lovely Woodland* walks!" over and over.

"You've only been doing this job for five minutes," said MacDuffy. "I've been a guard since I was a boy."

"You're only 16," Pie pointed out.

"Which is a pretty ripe old age for a Great City Guard," replied MacDuffy.

"I'm beginning to understand why," said Pie. He found a part of the wall where the bricks jutted out enough to act as footholds, and began to climb.

"What are you doing? That's not allowed. We have to stay down here and stand guard. Didn't you do the training?"

"What training?" replied Pie. "Yesterday, Commander Nelson handed me that spear and told me to stand outside the city wall and defend the city."

"Yep. That was the training," said MacDuffy. "You'll have noticed he made no mention of climbing walls. That's because it's not part of the job."

One of the bricks crumbled under Pie's right foot. He slipped and banged his chin but managed to hang onto the wall. "I'm climbing up so I can see what's going on," he said.

Most of the kingdom's towns were built on high ground that allowed them a good view of approaching enemies. The Great City, however, was in the middle of a forest. It was entirely surrounded by a high ridge that blocked the view from ground level.

"It's a very strange way to behave if you ask me," said MacDuffy. "What was your job before you became a guard?"

"I've had a lot of jobs but, most recently, I was an assistant to Desmond, the Dragon Dentist."

"Why have I heard that name?" enquired MacDuffy.

"He was eaten by a customer. Barry, the Town Crier, proclaimed it last week. I worked with him too."

"You worked with Barry the Town Crier who fell down a well?"

"Yes. Before that job, I was cleaning the sewers," said Pie.

"I thought all the sewer cleaners got eaten by those giant rats."

"All but one of them," Pie called down. He was now halfway up the wall. He could hear the city folk on the other side. Usually, this would just be the cheery calls of market stall owners, but today the shouts sounded more urgent.

"Before the sewers, I was an apprentice at the metalworks," continued Pie, shouting louder as he climbed.

"The metalworks that exploded?!" exclaimed MacDuffy.

"Yes, luckily I was down at the river collecting water at the time."

"Have you ever worked with anyone who has … well, survived?" called up MacDuffy, feeling suddenly nervous.

"Oh yes," said Pie. "Mantini is always with me and she's fine."

MacDuffy looked around, confused. "Who's Mantini? It's just you and me here."

Pie paused and turned his head. MacDuffy noticed that there were two eyes hidden behind the large white feather on top of Pie's hat. A small, pointed nose appeared and a brown mouse waved at him.

"Ah!" yelped MacDuffy. "A rodent!"

Pie reached the top of the wall, allowing him to finally see what the lookout was shouting about.

"Oh, I see. Lovely Woodland walks."

"Now, *you're* saying it," said MacDuffy.

"Yes, this looks bad. We're under attack," said Pie.

"Which of our many enemies is approaching? Whoever they are, I shall stand my ground. There is a reason I'm the longest-serving member of the City Guards. Whether it is the Armed Elephant Clan from the east or the Trout Tickling Tribes from the west, they shall perish by my spear … I say, I'd never noticed those bushes on top of the ridge."

"Those aren't bushes," said Pie. "They're treetops."

To his horror, MacDuffy saw that the surrounding forest had come to life and was now walking towards the city. A willow tree spun around and lobbed a huge boulder through the air. It crashed into the lookout tower, taking a huge chunk out of the side. Clouds of dust rose into the air, and the screams from the city got even louder.

"What wizardry is this?" MacDuffy grabbed Pie's discarded weapon and held both spears out in front of him.

"That might be the first sensible thing you've said during our brief time working together," said Pie.

"Brief?" said MacDuffy. "It's not over yet. We are guards. No matter the peril. No matter the enemy! I shall stand and fight and … oh dear. There really are a lot of trees, aren't there? They do look rather angry."

He glanced at Pie and immediately turned pale. "Er … w-where are you going?" stammered MacDuffy.

"Anywhere but here," replied Pie, and he dropped down the other side of the wall, leaving MacDuffy holding both spears as the trees approached.

Chapter 2

Agnes Magpie

The Great City was panicking. The citizens were running around, waving their arms in the air and screaming. Pie walked at a brisk pace, but did not run, as he knew that running was never a good idea in these situations. When he reached the gate to the Royal Battle Rooms, he found it unguarded. It was no surprise since King Formby had always made it very clear that, in times of emergency, the official ruling was "Run! Save yourself!"

Pie entered the Battle Room, which was splendidly decorated with tapestries showing the king bravely fighting fearsome enemies. At first, he thought the room was empty, then he spotted King Formby quaking under a table.

"Wh-who are you?" quavered the king. "Where is my guard?"

"I am Pie Fortune. I believe the city is under attack from an evil wizard. We must act quickly to save it."

"What makes you think it is an evil wizard behind this attack?" asked the king.

Pie rolled his eyes. "Trees don't usually walk."

A cupboard door swung open and a large moustached man stepped out. He wore a red jacket covered in medals. "The lad is making sense," he said. "Duck!"

"What duck, Commander Nelson?" replied the king.

But Pie knew precisely what he meant. He dived behind a throne as a hundred round brown pellets rained in on them.

Once the attack was over, Commander Nelson got to his feet and picked up one of the pellets. He sniffed it, then took a small nibble out of the side.

"Hm, horse chestnuts. Yes, I fear that this young man is correct. A dark wizard is attempting to conquer our great city."

"Oh dear, what can be done?" cried the king.

"We must evacuate the city and assemble a team of your bravest warriors to find and arrest the wizard behind all this," said Pie.

"Yes, what he said," added Commander Nelson.

"How do we evacuate – ? Who can we send?" asked King Formby.

"Excellent questions," said Commander Nelson, turning to face Pie.

Pie sighed. "Evacuate everyone through the sewers."

"Won't that be a bit smelly?" said the king.

"Yes," said Pie. "Oh, and watch out for giant rats. Take the north tunnel. That will bring you out on the far side of the forest. You should be able to set up camp at the foot of the mountains."

"And what about the brave warriors?" said the king.

"Hm, we do have a bit of a shortage of those at the moment," said Commander Nelson. "All my bravest warriors are currently on a team-building away day."

"All of them?" exclaimed Pie.

"Yes, I'm afraid so. As soon as this attack began, I sent a messenger tortoise to order them back, but I fear that will be too late."

"A messenger tortoise?" cried Pie.

"Yes, the pigeons are all on strike again," sighed Commander Nelson.

"Striking pigeons," sobbed the king.

"Try not to get in a flap," said Pie. "What about involving a wizard? Is Supreme Mage Magnusson still your chief magical advisor? He'd know what to do."

"Unfortunately, Supreme Mage Magnusson left following a dispute over jelly."

"Jelly?" repeated Pie.

"Yes. I ordered him to make the royal jelly dance at my last birthday party. He said that party tricks were beneath him."

"What happened after that?" asked Pie.

"He stormed out and I had to do with ordinary non-dancing jelly," replied the king. "That was a shame, but it was still a fun party. I got lots of presents."

"I meant what happened to Supreme Mage Magnusson?" asked Pie, with an exasperated sigh.

"He was ordered to leave the city," said Commander Nelson.

"So who is your magical advisor now?" asked Pie.

"That would be Agnes," said Commander Nelson. "Agnes, please reveal yourself."

Pie looked around excitedly. "Is she invisible?"

"Actually, I'm in here." A trunk opened to reveal a girl around the same age as Pie wearing flowing robes covered in stars.

"Yes, Agnes is currently the most experienced wizard in the city," said the king.

Pie looked unconvinced. "How long have you been studying magic?"

"How long in years or in months?" she replied.

"Years."

"Almost one."

"Not even a year." Pie threw his arms up in exasperation. "What happened to all the other wizards?"

Agnes and Commander Nelson looked at the king, who shifted uncomfortably, then said, "Listen, I have a lot of parties. And what's the point of a party without a dancing jelly? How was I meant to know that wizards get huffy if you ask them to do things like that?"

"Well, it looks like it's just you two young people on this mission then," said Commander Nelson.

"Won't you come?" asked Pie.

"Much as I would love to join you, I'm afraid I can't," said Commander Nelson. "I have to … er … make sure the king is safe."

"And get everyone else out of the city?" suggested Pie.

"Oh, yes. And that."

A hailstorm of acorns pummelled the room. The army of trees had now reached the city walls.

"It's down to you brave young things. Agnes Magpie and … what was your name again?"

"Pie Fortune … and Mantini."

The mouse in Pie's hat saluted.

"Yes, I hereby name Sir Pie Fortune … and er, mouse, the protector knight of the Great City. Good luck. We're all counting on you."

"Thank you," said Pie.

"And in the unlikely event that you return alive, I shall throw a big party in your honour … with dancing jelly and everything."

Invisibility spell

Turn one average-sized
person invisible for
around two hours.

Ingredients:

one beetroot

(medium-sized)

three frog ankles

(if none available,
use toad knees)

tears of a deer

one tablespoon

(boil first)   (heaped)

of grated dragon tooth

the sigh of a cow*

(Must be a cow. Not a bull!
Don't make that mistake again.)

Spelling spell

One cup of this potion
and you'll never misspell
a word again.

Ingredients:

two ~~clothes~~ *cloves* of garlic

~~hare~~ *hair* of a ~~hair~~ *hare*

pencil ~~led~~ *lead*

~~ferry~~ *fairy* dust

Chapter 3

A pantomime bush

King Formby and Commander Nelson ran off in one direction, while Pie and Agnes turned right at the palace gates.

"Shouldn't we escape through the sewers as well?" asked Agnes.

"No, we need to go through the front gates." Another tower came crashing to the ground as the trees stormed into the city. "Or whatever's left of them," added Pie.

"But why?"

"Because this city is surrounded by trees, but they are only attacking from that direction, which means the wizard behind all this is most likely over there. Now, what magic spells do you have that might help us?"

Agnes opened her book and then flicked through a few pages. "I've got spells for invisibility or invincibility. I always get those two mixed up."

"They both sound great," said Pie.

"Oh, except I don't have all of these ingredients."

"How many are you missing?"

Agnes checked her book. "Um ... one ... two ... er ... all of them ... I don't have a cauldron either."

Pie sighed. "So you can't do any spells?"

"Well, I can't exactly make the ingredients appear by magic, can I?" said Agnes.

"That's true," said Pie. "I know a little about magic myself. I once worked as Supreme Mage Magnusson's apprentice."

"Why did you give it up?" she asked.

"Too much stirring for my liking," said Pie.

"Yes, the stirring is a bit boring," she admitted, although in truth, it wasn't just the stirring Agnes struggled with. She simply wasn't a natural when it came to magic. She was always bottom of the class. She felt bad about this. Her father was a chimney sweep, who had worked long hours to send her to the Magic Academy.

Agnes had done her best to make the most of the opportunity, but she feared that her father was disappointed in her lack of progress.

Pie and Agnes stepped out onto the main street, where a large yew tree was spinning in circles, trying to catch a pigeon, and trampling on a number of smaller bushes with his large clomping roots.

"Hey, I've got an idea," said Pie.

Agnes followed him over to one of the fallen bushes, while a battalion of silver birches looted a clothes shop. Some of them were trying on various items of clothing. When Pie reached the squashed bush, he crouched down beside it.

"Quickly. We need to put this on."

"Put this bush on what?" replied Agnes.

"On us."

"Oh, as a disguise. Good plan."

Agnes and Pie lifted the bush and placed it over their heads. Thorns scratched their skin. Leaves tickled their knees. It was extremely uncomfortable but, after a bit of readjusting, they arranged it so they were both hidden inside the bush, with their feet on the ground.

"With me. Right foot. Left foot," said Pie.

"Why do I get the impression you've done this before?" asked Agnes.

"I worked briefly as the back half of a pantomime horse."

"That's the worst half, isn't it?"

"Usually, yes, but in this case, the scenery that fell onto the stage landed on the front half."

"I see." Agnes gulped, realising that she was at the front. "Where are we going?"

"Just keep walking," said Pie. "And I don't think we should talk. That cherry tree by the gate keeps giving us funny looks."

It wasn't the only one. The disguise was working with the larger trees, but the shrubs and other bushes kept glancing at them, sensing something wrong. Pie and Agnes sped up, walking as fast as possible until they got to the top of the ridge that surrounded the city. There were no trees on the other side, so they discarded the bush disguise.

"Did you know this ridge was actually put here by a previous king?" said Pie.
"About a hundred years ago, rocks and soil were carried from the surrounding mountains to make it."

"But it blocks the view. Why would you put it here on purpose?" replied Agnes.

"He wanted a moat, but the builders had the plans upside down."

They joined a rocky path that had once woven its way through the forest, but now stretched all the way to the mountain range across a barren landscape.

"How do you know all this stuff?" asked Agnes.

"I used to work for the Royal Society of Historians."

"Didn't they all get lost on a quest to find the lost city?"

"Well, no, they found that," said Pie. "They just couldn't find their way back. I got lucky and hitched a ride on the back of a giant migrating bat."

"A giant migrating bat. Oh, wow!" said Agnes, impressed.

"Yes, I learnt how to catch them when I was working at the Royal Institute of – "

"Halt. Who goes there!" The voice boomed from behind a large boulder.

Agnes stopped. "Uh-oh. Bandits!"

"No," said Pie. "Bandits actually have deep voices. This is someone putting on a deep voice."

"No, I am not," said the voice, with a threatening CLANK of a sword.

"He's armed," said Agnes. "Maybe we should go the other way."

"Nonsense," said Pie. "His voice has an echo, which means he's speaking into something to make it louder. From the sound of the clanking, that's copper, not steel. This is no sword-wielding bandit. It's a nervous boy with a lot of kitchenware."

"You will live to regret that." The owner of the voice leapt out, brandishing two large saucepans. Around his belt was a ladle, a couple of wooden spoons and a copper teapot with a long spout.

The Office of Peacekeeping's Most Wanted list

Beryl the Bandit Queen

The most successful bandit of all. It is now thought that most citizens of the Great City have been robbed by Beryl at some point.

Most likely to steal: everything and anything

Most likely to say: "Bow down before Beryl and hand over your goods!"

Reward: **500** gold coins

Roberta the Ruby Robber

Probably the pickiest of all bandits, Roberta only steals rubies. If it's a diamond, pearl, sapphire or even gold, she's not bothered.

Most likely to steal: rubies

Most likely to say: "Sapphires are blue, rubies are red, hand over your rubies or get a knock to the head."

Reward: **150** gold coins

Dan the Dandy Bandit

Winner of the best-dressed bandit five years running, Dan is not to be trifled with.

Most likely to steal: clothes / jewellery

Most likely to say: "You lot haven't got anything worth stealing. Sometimes, I don't know why I bother."

Reward: **200** gold coins

Chapter 4

The Dreaded Hood

"So you're a bandit, are you?" asked Pie, looking doubtfully at the pans in the boy's hands. "What's your plan then? Fry us like eggs?"

"These pans are deadly weapons in the hands of – " He paused, grabbed the teapot then spoke into the spout, making his voice sound bigger and more dramatic. "THE DREADED HOOD."

"What a ridiculous name," said Agnes. "You don't even have a hood, let alone a dreaded one."

"I've never heard of you," said Pie.

"Then you clearly don't work for the law." The boy laughed and slapped his thigh. "The police are always trying to catch … THE DREADED HOOD."

"Actually, I did briefly have a job as a secretary at the Office of Peacekeeping," said Pie. "There was Dan the Dandy Bandit, Roberta the Ruby Robber and, of course, Beryl the Bandit Queen, but I don't remember seeing your name on the Most Wanted list."

"I'm wanted just as much as Beryl," said the boy, sticking his tongue out. "Look. I've got a wanted poster and everything."

He clipped his pans onto his belt and pulled out a rather shoddily-made poster offering a reward of 5,000 gold coins for the capture of the Dreaded Hood.

"You made that yourself," said Pie.

"I did not."

"Yes, you did. Look at the bottom, you wrote *I* instead of *he*."

WANTED The Dreaded Hood
The most fearsum villan in the hole of Lovely Woodland
For crime that I committed against the Great City
Reward: 5,000 Gold Coins

The boy looked at the poster, realised this was true, then quickly rolled it back up again.

"Listen, just hand over your loot or else."

"Or else you'll hit us with a saucepan?" said Agnes.

"Exactly."

"We don't have any loot," said Pie. "We're on our way to find the evil wizard who made the trees attack the city."

"Oh, is that what's happened?" said the boy. "I thought maybe they were taking a holiday."

"Trees don't take holidays," said Pie.

"If they did, they'd have to remember to pack their trunks," joked Agnes.

Pie rolled his eyes. "Listen, why don't you come with us?" he said to the boy. "We need someone like you by our side."

"You mean, because of my weaponry and unmatched battle skills?"

"Absolutely," said Pie. "But also because we'll probably need to eat at some point so the pots and pans will come in handy. And you never know when you might need a ladle."

The boy considered before replying. "Yes, I shall join you. It's very hard to do any proper looting and robbing without trees, anyway. There's not really anywhere good to hide."

"What's your name?" asked Pie. "After all, we can't keep calling you the Dreaded Hood."

"Claymore," said the boy.

"Pleased to meet you. This is Agnes Magpie and I am Pie Fortune. Now, let's go and find the wizard behind this mischief."

The three brave adventurers continued on their way. They marched across the barren plain until they reached the village of *Rather* at the base of *Done Hill*, beside the river *Bottom*. The sign at the village entrance read: Rather Under Done on the Bottom.

"Hm, it all looks a bit quiet, doesn't it?" said Pie.

"Perhaps the trees attacked the village before advancing on the Great City," said Agnes.

"Yes, but look at this barley field," said Pie. "If the trees had come this way, they would have trampled over it. No, there's something wrong here."

"Whatever dangers lie ahead, my trusty weapons and I will keep you safe." Claymore glared around him as if he had razor-sharp cutlasses rather than a pair of grubby saucepans. But he almost jumped out of his skin when three burly villagers stepped out of a nearby door, holding pitchforks.

"Be gone," yelled the burliest of the three men.

"Yes, we don't want your kind around here," said the one to his left.

"Yeah," agreed the man on the right.

"We're looking for a wizard," said Pie.

"We don't have one of those," replied the man on the left.

"Isn't the guy in the tower a wizard?" said the one on the right.

"No," said the man in the middle. "He's a wise man and he keeps us safe. He warned us people like you would come. Your city is being destroyed so now you want to come and take our village."

"That's not it at all," said Pie. "You said this wise man keeps you safe. What from?"

"Dragon attacks."

"Dragons have attacked the village?" said Pie. "I hadn't heard that."

"Well, no. They haven't because our wise man has kept them away," said the middle man.

Pie winked at Agnes. "Ah, right. So what other unseen horrors has he kept you safe from?"

"There was that flood that never happened," said the one of the left.

"And the plague of locusts he stopped," said the one on the right.

"Plagues of bees, birds, illnesses … squirrels," continued the middle one. "Pretty much, you name it, that wise man in the tower has stopped it happening."

"And what proof do you have that any of this would have happened anyway?" asked Pie.

"We don't go in for proving things here in the village of Rather," said the one in the middle.

"That's right," said the man to the right. "As long as it sounds likely, it's probably true. That's our motto."

"And does it sound likely that all these terrible plagues were prevented by this mysterious man in the tower?" asked Pie.

"Now you mention it, not that likely," he admitted.

"I think we'd like to speak to this wise man of yours," said Pie.

The Dreaded Hood's Guide to Combat

The Saucepan Block

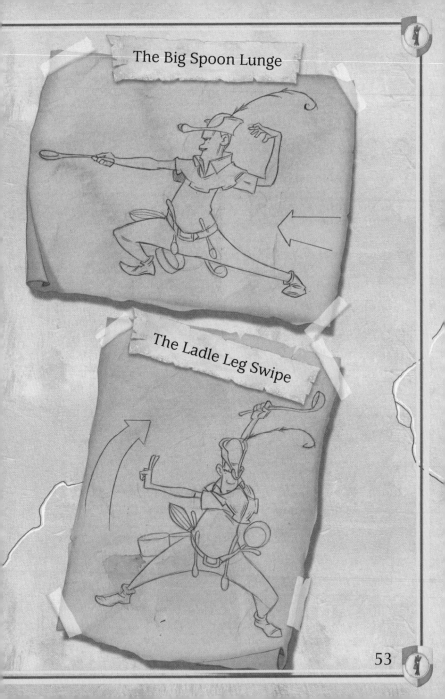

The Big Spoon Lunge

The Ladle Leg Swipe

Chapter 5

Tigers and spaghetti

The stone tower cast a long shadow across the village. Clouds of colourful smoke billowed from the window at the top.

"Now, that's what I call an evil wizard's lair," said Pie.

"You won't be able to reach him," warned the burliest villager. "Even if you got past the tigers, you would have to break his protection spell and then climb the unclimbable stairs."

"Right," said Pie. "So tigers, protection spell and unclimbable stairs. I think we'd better do some shopping before we take on this wizard. Where's your village shop?"

The three burly men pointed to a building, with a sign outside that read: STUFF-U-NEED.

"Thanks," said Pie. "Come on then."

When Pie, Agnes and Claymore entered the shop, a bell rang, and a bearded shopkeeper jumped up from behind the counter.

"How can I help you?" he said.

"We're looking for these things." Pie handed the shopkeeper a piece of parchment.

"You want a piece of paper with some squiggles on it?" The shopkeeper looked at it, confused.

"Er, no. That's a list of … it doesn't matter," said Pie. "We need a bag of apples and some rope."

"The apples are by the window, but we don't sell rope," said the shopkeeper. "There's no money in it."

"Do you sell spaghetti?" asked Pie.

"Yes," replied the shopkeeper.

"In which case, we need all of your spaghetti," said Pie. "And Agnes would like to see your witches' section."

"It's at the end of the aisle," said the shopkeeper. "I hope you can pay for all this."

Agnes went to find ingredients while Claymore helped Pie to find the spaghetti.

"But we haven't got any money," said Claymore.

"True. I'll have to pay with your teapot," whispered Pie.

"This old thing? It's not worth very much," replied Claymore, handing Pie the teapot.

"Oh, don't worry about that," Pie winked.

Claymore handed Pie the teapot, then
went to find apples. Agnes filled a basket with
magical ingredients while Pie spoke quietly
to the shopkeeper. Once they had everything
they needed, they all left the shop, leaving
the shopkeeper eagerly rubbing the teapot.

"I can't believe he accepted a rusty old
teapot as payment," said Claymore.

"I told him it was a magic wishing teapot,"
said Pie. "He's expecting a genie to pop out
and grant him three wishes. People round
here really will believe anything. Now, let's
get cooking. I'll need both your pans."

"Both? What for?" asked Claymore.

"One for Agnes's magic spell," replied Pie. "The other to cook this spaghetti."

Agnes set to work brewing the potion, while Claymore fetched water from the river. Pie lit a fire. Once the spaghetti was cooked, he and Claymore sat down to weave it together into a long piece of rope.

"So what now?" asked Claymore.

"Now, we scale the tower and defeat the evil wizard. Agnes, how's the potion looking?" Pie peered over and looked at the bubbling liquid, which had turned the colour of pondweed. "Is it supposed to look like that?"

"I don't know," said Agnes. "I've never made it before."

"Let's hope it works then," said Pie.

Once everything was ready, Agnes picked up the cauldron, Claymore carried the spaghetti and Pie grabbed the bag of apples, and all three of them marched to the highest point of the village where the rickety tower stood. It was surrounded by a fence. Inside the fence were ten large snarling tigers.

"So, what's the plan?" asked Agnes. "Are the apples poisoned?"

"There's no need for that," said Pie. "Look."

He walked to the far corner of the fence and poured the bag of apples into the yard. Instantly, the tigers clambered over each other as they all rushed to eat the apples, leaving the path free. "I learnt how much tigers love apples while I was working for a travelling circus. That's where I met Mantini."

The mouse on Pie's hat performed a triple somersault, landed, rolled over, squeaked "Ta-da!" and then bowed.

"The travelling circus was destroyed by a tornado," said Agnes.

"Yes, and if it hadn't been for Mantini, I'd have been a goner too," he replied. "But that's another story."

"Enough chatting. Let's go," said
Claymore, charging up the path and grabbing
the door handle. As soon as his hand touched
the building, he was thrown backwards. A few
tigers glanced up at him briefly but they were
more interested in the apples.

"You can't touch the tower until the protection
spell has been removed," said Pie.

"I thought Agnes's potion got rid of the protection spell," replied Claymore.

"She hasn't said the magic words yet," said Pie.

"Oh right, yes." Agnes flicked to the right page in her book. "Here we are … Shim Shala Shear. Make this spell disappear."

With a CLICK the door swung open, revealing a winding staircase.

"Excellent job," said Pie. "Now, I wonder what makes it unclimbable."

"Let's see." Claymore bounded forwards to try the staircase. The first step crumbled as soon as his foot touched it, and he slid back down. Claymore landed with a thump.

"Hand me the spaghetti rope," said Pie.

Pie tied a knot in the end to make it into a lasso. After a few swings, he threw it up so that it caught on the top of the tower.

"Wow!" said Claymore. "Where did you learn that?"

"I used to work on a cattle farm," said Pie. "Just before the great cattle plague. Now, let's get climbing and put an end to this."

The Incredible Mantini!

Marvel at the somersaults and
death-defying trapeze stunts
performed by the world's most
INCREDIBLE ACROBATIC MOUSE,
and witness her fly
through the terrifying …
RING OF FIRE!

Chapter 6

The disgruntled wizard

Pie climbed the spaghetti rope, with Agnes and Claymore close behind. Mantini peered over the rim of Pie's hat at them.

"Be very careful when you reach the top," warned Pie. "Who knows what magical trickery we will find up here?"

At the top, they hauled themselves inside the tower. They landed inside a circular room full of cauldrons, all brimming with bubbling liquid.

"Wow, look at all these spells," said Agnes.

"And this must be our evil wizard," said Pie, spotting the figure of a man through the dense smoke. Pie was expecting to see a wizard with a long beard and cloak, but the man who stood in front of them wore tatty black trousers and shirt. He held a long brush and had soot all over his face. He looked more like a chimney sweep than a wizard.

"Dad?" said Agnes.

"Yes, my dear, and what a disappointment it is that you have wasted the education that I worked so hard to pay for."

"But … but … I'm the king's chief magical advisor," said Agnes.

"Pah! Only because all the good wizards were either sacked or left because of that awful king."

"But … but – " Agnes looked like she was going to cry. "I'm sorry."

"That isn't your father," said Pie. "It's the wizard in disguise."

Immediately, there was a huge puff of smoke and the chimney sweep was gone. In his place stood a strong woman, dressed in leather, wearing a crown and carrying an axe.

"Who are you?" demanded Agnes.

"Now, she looks familiar," said Pie.

"It's B-b-b-Beryl the B-b-b-bandit Queen," stammered Claymore.

"That's right," snarled the fearsome woman. "And you are no bandit, Claymore. You're a weakling."

"Oh, I see what's going on," said Pie. "This sorcerer is showing us the things we most fear. For Agnes, that's disappointing her father, whereas Claymore is scared that he's not ferocious enough to be a real bandit."

"I'm not," protested Claymore.

There was another puff of smoke and Beryl the Bandit Queen was gone, only to be replaced by a rat the size of a human. The three friends jumped back in disgust and knocked over a cauldron. The rat changed again. This time, there was a long-bearded man crouching like a rat and twitching his nose.

"My old boss, Supreme Mage Magnusson," gasped Pie. "So you're the evil wizard behind all this mayhem."

"Hello, Pie, you always were one of my brighter apprentices, but I'm not evil. I'm merely disgruntled."

"The game is up," declared Pie. "You have to stop the trees attacking the city. We were sent by King Formby himself."

"What? That fool of a king?" scoffed Mage Magnusson. "I'd rather eat a toenail sandwich than work for him again. I tell you what, you seem like three bright young people. How about, instead of arresting me, we go back to the Great City and put you lot in charge? Agnes, you may continue in your role as chief magical advisor. Claymore, you would make a superb new commander of the armies and, as for you, Pie, you could be the new prime minister."

"I do think I'm getting better at magic all the time," said Agnes.

"And I like the sound of being in charge of armies," said Claymore.

"Don't be fooled," said Pie. "Tell us, Mage Magnusson, what role would you have in this new order?"

"I was thinking I'd make a rather good king," he said.

"You see," said Pie. "He's just trying to win you over by appealing to the thing we all most desire."

"But how does he know about our fears and desires in the first place?" asked Claymore.

"From all these magic spells, of course," said Pie. "Come on."

Pie tipped over one of the cauldrons, spilling the potion.

"Noo! No! Stop!" cried Mage Magnusson, but it was too late. Pie, Agnes and Claymore were all tipping over cauldrons, sending the stinky, colourful liquid splurging out. Within a matter of minutes, every cauldron was upturned and empty.

Pie ran to the window and looked towards the city. As he'd hoped, the trees were now making their way back to the forest.

"We've done it!" said Agnes. "We've saved the Great City!"

"What now?" asked Claymore.

"Now we take this traitor back to face trial," said Pie.

"That's what you think," said Mage Magnusson, and he pulled out from his pocket a tiny pot, barely bigger than a thimble.

"Oh no, he's got a travel cauldron," said Agnes.

"Yes, I'm always prepared for a quick getaway," said Mage Magnusson, "and I always carry this vanishing spell with me."

"All he has to do is say the magic words and he'll be gone," said Agnes.

"Claymore, hand me a ladle," said Pie.

Claymore did as he was told. Pie took it and threw it with precise aim. Mage Magnusson was in the middle of muttering the magic words when the ladle hit the cauldron with a PING and sent the contents all over the wizard.

"You did it!" said Agnes.

"Er, I half did it," said Pie.

Mage Magnusson's spell had begun
to work. His legs had vanished but his top
half remained.

"Mage Magnusson, you are under arrest,"
said Pie. "Or your top half is."

"You will stand trial for what you've done,"
said Claymore.

"Yes, and you haven't got a leg to stand on,"
said Agnes.

And so it was that Pie Fortune, Agnes
Magpie and Claymore the Dreaded Hood saved
the Great City.

The End

The three heroes!

PIE FORTUNE

INTELLIGENCE: 9/10

MAIN STRENGTH: Intelligence/wit

BIGGEST FEAR: Giant sewer rats

AGNES MAGPIE
INTELLIGENCE: 6/10
STRENGTH: Magic (when it works)
BIGGEST FEAR: Disappointing her father

CLAYMORE (THE DREADED HOOD)
INTELLIGENCE: 4/10
STRENGTH: Fighting
BIGGEST FEAR: Beryl the Bandit Queen

Dragon Dentist Assistant

Cattle Farmhand

Great City Guard

Barry the Town Crier's Helper

Apprentice at Metalworks

Sewage Worker

Secretary, Office of Peacekeeping

Wizard's Apprentice

Circus Sawdust Sweeper

Bag Carrier, Royal Society
of Historians

Librarian, the Royal Institute
of Unlikely Animals

Pantomime Horse
(back half)

Official Royal Guidelines
of what to do in a crisis

1. HIDE!

2. If you have nowhere to hide ... RUN!

3. If you have nowhere to run . . . PANIC!

4. If you are too scared to panic . . . HIDE!

* Please note, your king will probably have hidden
or run away.

About the author

A bit about me …

My name is Gareth P Jones.
I am an award-winning author
and performer. I have written over
45 books for children of all ages,
ranging from picture books to older,
stranger, and sometimes scarier
novels. I also spend a lot of time
visiting schools and festivals where
I sing songs about my books.

Gareth P Jones

Why did you want to be an author?

I like making things up, using my imagination, and
escaping into stories. One way to do this is to read.
Another is to write. I love writing. I have things I want to
share. Some of them are funny things. Some of them are
strange and silly. A few of them are scary. When I share
them, I feel more connected to the world and life makes
more sense.

What is it like for you to write?

It varies day to day. At the moment, I am a bit obsessed with
writing songs. I pretty much write a song a day – about all
sorts of things. But I've just finished a novel about cats and I'm
working on a picture book that I had an idea for yesterday.

86

What book do you remember loving reading when you were young?

The one that sticks in my memory is *The Phantom Tollbooth* by Norton Juster. It's full of wonderful wordplay and it demonstrates that you can never be bored if you have an enquiring mind and a good imagination.

Why did you write this book?

I have always loved fantasy stories about brave knights and evil wizards. I was delighted to have the opportunity to write one of my own. I'd like to write more now.

Is there anything in this book that relates to your own experiences?

Yes, I also once worked as a dragon dentist's assistant. There's a plaque somewhere … we scraped it off the dragon's teeth.

What do you hope readers will get out of the book?

I hope they will laugh and then dream about going on madcap adventures of their own.

Would you rather be a wizard or a knight?

I'd rather be a wizard, but I don't think I'd be a very good wizard as I'm not very good at following instructions. I'm a terrible baker and I think wizardry would be like that, but with more dire consequences than a soggy-bottomed flan if it goes wrong.

About the illustrator

What made you want to be an illustrator?

Dan Whisker

As a child I was always interested in drawing, especially Greek mythology. I loved all of the monsters, heroes and fantastical stories. I used my mum's grease-proof cooking paper to trace all of the wonderful characters and creatures. That's how I learnt to draw, learning to see images in shapes.

What did you like best about illustrating this book?

My favourite thing about illustrating this book was both the humour in the story and the variety of illustrations. I got to draw a mix of small pictures, big scenes and maps. I was able to use my imagination to visualise the world of Pie Fortune!

Is there anything in this book that relates to your own experiences?

I can relate to Claymore in this book, especially when it comes to climbing. I have always had a fear of heights!

When I visited the Eiffel Tower in Paris, I spent most of my time clinging for dear life to the inner railing – much to my wife's amusement!

How do you bring a character to life?

The first thing I do is read the book several times to really know the characters and the writer's voice. I look at the briefs and for any written description of the character, either physical or their personality. Then I draw several concept designs until I create a character that feels right.

Which character did you most like illustrating?

I enjoyed the character Claymore. He really tries hard to impress people, but it's not really him. He just needs to be himself and learn he is liked and accepted just the way he is. I enjoyed tinkering around a bit with Claymore's facial features. He has a long face and a buck tooth, so I made him look a little goofy!

Pie Fortune in the story has had a lot of interesting jobs. What's the strangest job you've ever done?

As a teenager I applied for a little job on a farm, pickling eggs and packing them to make some pocket money to keep me in art materials! Unfortunately, it only lasted a day after a giant pickled egg fight erupted. I was not asked to come back!

Book chat

Which character did you like best, and why?

What do the three heroes learn on their adventure?

If you could give the author one piece of advice to improve the book, what would it be?

Does the book remind you of any other books you've read? How?

Would you like to read another book about Pie and his friends? If so, what might it be about?

If you could talk to one character who would you pick? What would you say to them?

Which scene stands out most for you? Why?

What different skills do you think Pie, Agnes and Claymore have? Do they make a good team?

Book challenge:

Think of the most bizarre job that you'd like to do and list the skills you'd need.

Collins
BIG CAT

Published by Collins
An imprint of HarperCollins*Publishers*

The News Building
1 London Bridge Street
London SE1 9GF
UK

Macken House
39/40 Mayor Street Upper
Dublin 1
D01 C9W8
Ireland

Download the teaching notes and
word cards to accompany this book at:
http://littlewandle.org.uk/signupfluency/

British Library Cataloguing-in-Publication Data
A catalogue record for this publication is available
from the British Library.

Get the latest Collins Big Cat news at
collins.co.uk/collinsbigcat

Author: Gareth P Jones
Illustrator: Dan Whisker (The Bright Agency)
Publisher: Lizzie Catford
Product manager and
  commissioning editor: Caroline Green
Series editor: Charlotte Raby
Development editor: Catherine Baker
Project manager: Emily Hooton
Content editor: Daniela Mora Chavarría
Copyeditor: Sally Byford
Proofreader: Gaynor Spry
Cover designer: Sarah Finan
Typesetter: 2Hoots Publishing Services Ltd
Production controller: Katharine Willard

Collins would like to thank the teachers and
children at the following schools who took part in
the trialling of Big Cat for Little Wandle Fluency:
Burley And Woodhead Church of England Primary
School; Chesterton Primary School; Lady Margaret
Primary School; Little Sutton Primary School;
Parsloes Primary School.

Printed and bound in the UK using 100% Renewable
Electricity at Martins the Printers Ltd

MIX
Paper | Supporting
responsible forestry
FSC www.fsc.org
FSC™ C007454